Get Acquainted with God

By Kenneth Hagin Jr.

Chapter 1
KNOWING THE FATHER

Acquaint now thyself with him, and be at peace: thereby good shall come unto thee.
— Job 22:21

Our text talks about getting acquainted with God. I like it best in *The Amplified Bible:* "Acquaint now yourself with Him [agree with God and show yourself to be conformed to His will] and be at peace; by that [you shall prosper and great] good shall come to you.''

As I traveled this summer, preaching, I found that if there's any cry on the hearts of God's people it's a cry for a mighty move of God. But if we are to have a supernatural move of God, we first must get acquainted with God. We must know and understand who He is.

First, we must realize that God is a spirit. We hear this; we tritely talk about it; and we literally agree to it sometimes. But we need to realize that God, who is a spirit, is omnipresent: He is present everywhere all of the time, existing everywhere simultaneously.

When we begin to think like that, it's almost beyond the scope of our intellect. How can we think of Someone who is present *everywhere*, filling every corner of this universe we live in? That means He is just the same in Kenya as He is right now in Tulsa. That is a staggering thought!

We can understand an individual's being in a certain place at a certain time. But God, who is a spirit, is in the United States and in Kenya at the same time He's in South Africa, in Australia, in India, in Belgium, and in Germany — and He's just as powerful there as He is here. Now that is an awesome thought!

It is almost beyond our understanding, in fact, to comprehend a Being who is present everywhere and has the same power everywhere. Some will respond, "I never thought of that before. I never thought of God in that magnitude before. I thought of Him as a King on a throne."

Suddenly you begin to realize that this omnipresent Spirit of God who is the same all over the world also is communing with you and me on a one-to-one basis. We think about the awesomeness of God. We think about the power of God. We think about how big God is. Yes, God is all of that, but we also must realize that God is as personal with us as He is with every other one of His children. That is a tremendous thought!

My two children must be physically where I am if they're going to be in my presence. All of God's children can be in His presence all the time everywhere they are. That's how big God is.

We need to get acquainted with God on those terms — in the intimacy of a Father-child relationship — not just in the awesome fact of His greatness.

John 4:24 says, *"God is a Spirit: and they that worship him must worship him in spirit and in truth."*

You must realize that you are a spirit; you have a *soul*; and you live in a *body*. You cannot understand God with your intellect. That's what's wrong with the world today: People have tried to understand God and the things of God with their minds. That's why you see empty words with no power and no supernatural manifestations in so many churches. People are trying to understand God with the intellect.

Yes, in my office on the RHEMA Bible Training Center campus and in my study at home I have textbook after textbook, many huge, written by people who have many degrees after their names. All of them talk about God and His family — but they're explaining it from a theological standpoint.

Oh, you'll learn a little from these books, but you'll never know God from them! You can study every theology book that's ever been written, but you'll still never know God from them. You'll know something *about* God, but you'll never *know* God.

You will never get acquainted with God

until your spirit comes in contact with God's Spirit. Then you'll get acquainted with God.

The decision of how well you get acquainted with your heavenly Father rests with you, because it's your spirit that has to be in full contact with God — not your mind, not what you hear, not what you see, not what you read — but your spirit coming in contact with God's Spirit. That's where the real knowledge of God takes place.

Furthermore, you can't understand God with your emotions. Many people think faith is when you "feel good." No, *faith is not emotion; faith produces emotion.* There's a big difference!

You charismatics shouldn't look down on the old Pentecostals for clapping and singing until they felt good, because you've developed some of the same habits! Some charismatics do it, too. They have to "work up" until they get in the sing-song rhythm. So let's stop putting ourselves in these "boxes" and thinking it's got to be done one way or another.

Let's get acquainted with God and realize that God has many ways of ministering to His people. When it's spontaneous worship, it's great, but when it's worked-up emotion, it's nothing but sounding brass and tinkling cymbal.

Chapter 2
SUPERNATURAL
VS. SPECTACULAR

When you're intimately acquainted with God, you'll quit looking for the spectacular, because you'll realize that *the supernatural is not the spectacular.*

If someone were to get out of a wheelchair miraculously during a service, word would get around, and you couldn't get all the people in the building the next night. Why? Because we humans, for some reason or other, prefer getting involved with the spectacular — with something in the emotional realm — instead of getting involved with God in our spirits.

We should get just as excited about God — and should jump just as high and have just as much excitement — whether we ever see anybody walk out of a wheelchair or not.

Knowing God and having the Spirit of God flow in you does not depend on how many people get healed. (To listen to some people, you would think they *had* to have somebody healed or delivered in a service — which is fine — but they have quit looking at God in the *supernatural* and have started looking at God in the *spectacular*.)

When you get out of the realm of worshipping God and letting things happen as they're supposed to, and you start coming to church to see who's going to get blessed and healed, then you're moving from one realm to another. That's why you don't see God work.

God does not work when people come to church expecting to see supernatural miracles. God works when people come together to worship Him in spirit and in truth and are not concerned about signs and wonders.

When people get acquainted with God and worship Him in spirit and in truth, the signs and wonders will happen. And when the modern Church gets its priorities straight, you talk about spectacular — the Early Church won't have anything on us!

God wants to move. God wants to do exactly what He said in His Word. But when a move of God starts, people quit worshipping God and start looking for the miraculous. That quenches the Holy Spirit and God can't operate.

The only evangelist mentioned in the Bible is Philip in the New Testament Book of Acts. After Philip preached Jesus to the people and ministered to them, the apostles, the teachers, and the pastors went out to take care of his converts, because people got saved and healed and wonders started happening.

I believe we're going to see that happen again in this last day as people get acquainted with God. We know about the offices of the pastor, the teacher, the apostle, and the prophet, for we have seen them. But in the last 28 years we have seen very little of the ministry of the evangelist.

I believe that as the Body of Christ begins to come together and realize how to become acquainted with God, we will see the return of the evangelist as never before. And you talk about a move of God — there will be a move of God!

Pastors and teachers have taught the Word and taught the Word and taught the Word, creating a foundation for the evangelists to build upon in soul-winning, because the pastors and teachers can take care of those won into the kingdom by the evangelists.

We also must understand that God is the Creator. He is the I AM. He is, was, and forever will be the same. It is written in Malachi 3:6, *"I am the Lord, I change not."*

If He is the Lord and He changes not, then why are we, His children, getting excited and upset over the present-day economic recession? God says, *"I am the Lord, I change not."*

In studying the Pentateuch, the first five books of the Bible, I've learned that God raised up some children long ago; actually, they were the children of Abraham by physical descent. Then I found from studying Galatians 3 that you and I have become the spiritual sons of Abraham and thus the children of God, adopted into His family, and as such we have every right and privilege the blood descendants had.

I also read how God took care of His
children. When they had nothing to eat,
He gave them food to eat. He took care of
their clothing. He took care of everything
they needed. God is still the same today!
He is the same God who told Moses, "Tell
Pharaoh that I AM sent you."

There aren't enough demons in hell,
there is no sickness, there is no economic
condition that can keep the children of
God down when they know who their
heavenly Father is — when they are
acquainted with God. There is no way they
can be defeated. They are successes and
conquerors in Christ Jesus. That's what
Paul said, writing under the inspiration of
the Holy Spirit.

That's what happens when you get
acquainted with God; when you know He's
not just a Being sitting on a throne
somewhere "out there" in the ether.

Chapter 3
UNDERSTANDING
OUR INHERITANCE

So many of us talk about being "king's kids," but all we know is Jesus, our elder Brother. We've never really gotten acquainted with the King — God Himself — the Father. We can know who He is through knowing Him in our spirit: what He is, who He is, and why we're in existence.

Why did God create man? He created man to have someone to fellowship with — someone to give His inheritance to. That's what the Bible teaches. God said in Genesis 1:26, *"Let us make man in our image."* He made man to fellowship with.

Sometimes we get excited about the inheritance we have in God, but we don't know the Creator who gave it to us in the first place. We also must understand what that inheritance is: God has left us salvation, according to John 3:16.

JOHN 3:16
16 For God so loved the world, that he gave his only begotten Son, that whosoever believeth in Him should not perish, but have everlasting life.

Knowing that God is love is getting acquainted with God. He is so much, and He loved us so much, that He gave.

When you get acquainted with God, you will not be concerned any longer about the "big I" and what "I" can get. You will be concerned about those who are lost, dying, sick, and entrapped in satanic bondage.

When you know who God really is, your cries and prayers will not be, "God bless me and mine." You'll quit praying for God to bless you. You'll begin to pray for God to meet the needs of others.

There's just something about it: When you start acting like the Father and start being concerned about others instead of yourself, you will realize one day that everything you need and want has already been taken care of.

Let's look at that from a natural standpoint. I am a son of a fantastic man of God. As I grew up, I began to give of myself to help take care of the family, the cars, the yard, and the house. I didn't do it because I was told, "Son, go mow the yard, do this, do the other." No, when I saw that the garage need cleaning out, I cleaned out the garage. When I saw that the yard needed mowing, I mowed the yard. When I saw that the house needed painting, I got some paint and painted the house. When I saw the car needed washing, I didn't wash it only when I wanted to go on a date — no, I tried to take care of it all the time.

I noticed that when I began to do this, I didn't have to keep asking, "Dad, can I do this? Can I have that? I need this. I need that." I noticed that those things started being taken care of.

The Word of God says, *"If ye then, being evil, know how to give good gifts unto your children, how much more shall your Father which is in heaven give good things to them that ask him?"* (Matt. 7:11).

That's what happens when you get acquainted with God.

I am tremendously excited about enjoying the prosperity God can give us, yes — but I am more concerned about people being won into the kingdom of God. To me, that's more important than anything else.

I wish we would take the same confession and the same faith we're always using to confess and believe God for things for ourselves and band together and begin to confess and believe souls into the kingdom of God!

As we traveled in the summer of 1982, preaching across the United States, we saw more people saved in our meetings than ever before. One reason for this is because God dealt with Brother Hagin and me to begin to pray and believe for the salvation of souls — just like we believe for our budget to be met. You see, we can take the same principles we have learned for faith and use them to believe for the salvation of souls.

And when you get acquainted with God, you'll be more concerned with the lost than with yourself. I realize that a lot of people don't like to hear somebody preach like this, but if you seek first the kingdom of God, you don't have to worry about other things; they'll be added unto you (Matt. 6:33). Quit seeking things, and begin to seek the kingdom.

Jesus Christ also left us an inheritance of healing. First Peter 2:24 says, *"by whose* [His] *stripes ye WERE healed."* If ye *were*, then ye *are*. As a fellow said to me down in Texas, "If I *were*, then I *is."* (Now, I realize that's not good English, but I want to tell you, he got hold of it and got healed!)

Scholars can write all the theological books they want to against healing, but that fellow said, "If I *was* healed, then I *am* healed. Bless God, the Word says my Father said it; I don't care what anybody else says."

We've got to get to the point where we believe, like a little child does, that if Daddy said it, that's it. Nobody is ever going to tell him any different.

I remember as I was growing up, when my Father told me something, I believed him implicitly. And I know that after I've told my boy, Craig, something, 1,500 people could tell him it isn't so, but that boy would stand there and say, "Yeah, but I don't care what you say. My Daddy said . . . ."

I'm going to stand up and say the same thing: "Believe what you want; write what you want; do what you want; but my

heavenly Father said that I was healed!
I'm going to go by what my Father says!"
If you'll do that right now, you'll be healed
in your body.

God said in His Word that He has
given us all the desires of our heart. When
we get acquainted with God, we will know
that we can have all of our needs and
desires met: *"But my God shall supply all
your need according to his riches in glory
by Christ Jesus"* (Phil. 4:19).

MARK 11:23,24
23 For verily I say unto you, That whosoever shall
say unto this mountain, Be thou removed, and be thou
cast into the sea; and shall not doubt in his heart, but
shall believe that those things which he saith shall
come to pass; he shall have whatsoever he saith.
24 Therefore I say unto you, What things soever ye
desire, when ye pray, believe that ye receive them, and
ye shall have them.

You see, they're our inheritance.

Chapter 4
AGREEING WITH GOD

Once you get acquainted with God — once you know Him — you must *agree* with Him. That's what our text said: "Acquaint now yourself with Him [agree with God] . . . ." Agree with God. Too many people don't even agree with what God said. When you tell them what the Word says, they reply, "Yeah, but . . . ."

To get acquainted with somebody, you've got to listen to him; you've got to hear what he says. If you want to get acquainted with God, listen to Him; hear what He's saying. It's right here in the Word of God.

Can you get acquainted with somebody if the two of you sit down, say, "My name is Ken" and "My name is John," and stare at each other for three hours? How much are you going to know about John when you get up? How much is John going to know about Ken?

Well, John is going to know my name is Ken, and I'm going to know his name is John. That's about all we're going to know about one another except what we look like. But if we had sat there for three hours conversing back and forth with one another, we'd know something about each other.

To get acquainted with God, we've got to read His Word, find ourselves a place of prayer, and do some talking to Him — but not all the time. There are times we've got to be quiet and let Him talk a while.

A man came to me the other day and said, "I don't ever hear God talk to me."

I said, "Well, do you ever talk to Him?"

He said, "I talk to Him continually — all the time."

I said, "That's the problem. You never shut up long enough to listen!"

Get acquainted with God. Know Him. Know Him through the Word. Converse

with Him. And once you do, you've got to
agree with Him. This goes right back to
Matthew 18:19, where Jesus said, *"If two
of you shall AGREE on earth as touching
any thing that they shall ask, it shall be
done for them of my Father which is in
heaven."* What can happen then?
Anything! When you and God come into
agreement on this Word, heaven and earth
will move.

The Word says, *"Heaven and earth
shall pass away, but my words shall not
pass away"* (Matt. 24:35). That's God's
Word. Get acquainted with God and His
Word.

We sing a song sometimes that goes,
"Stand, stand, I cannot be defeated." I
don't care how many billows of life's sea
splash in my face. I don't care how many
times the devil reaches up and slaps me.
I cannot be defeated, because I have
agreed with God's Word. And God's Word
says I'm healed, whole, blessed, delivered,

and set free. I'm a conqueror in Christ Jesus.

I'm talking about getting acquainted with God to the point that you can stand your ground when everything around you looks bad.

Our text in *The Amplified Bible* says, "*show yourself to be conformed to His will.*" That means coming in line with what God said. If God said it, grab yourself by the back of the neck and say, "Come on over here, boy, and line up with God." Now, you may think that's a funny illustration, but sometimes you have to do that, because this old man — this old physical body — is still contacting this world, and it doesn't want to line up with God all the time. It wants to do this, that, or the other instead. And you must grab it, hold on, and say, "Come here, boy. This is what God said. Now get on this side of the fence and stay there. Line up with God!"

Chapter 5
BE AT PEACE

If you make a mistake and sin, ask for forgiveness. First John 1:9 says, *"If we confess our sins [ask for forgiveness], he is faithful and just to forgive us our sins, and to cleanse us from all unrighteousness."*

Oh, what a loving heavenly Father! Come on over and line up with God — really get acquainted with Him. Then, after acquainting yourself with Him, agreeing with Him, and being conformed to His will, be at peace. That's an important point: *Be at peace.*

You have to make yourself be at peace. You do it; God doesn't do it for you. You make yourself be at peace.

What does it mean to be at peace? It means don't think about what you're missing in the world. Don't think about what the economic system is going through.

Don't think about what the magazines and newspapers are saying. Be at peace.

A preacher asked me, "Are you traveling again this summer?"

I said, "Yes, we are."

He said, "I see you've got an 18-wheeler that says Kenneth Hagin Ministries on the side of it."

I said, "Yes, sir."

He said, "I see you're going to have that singing group go in one direction and you're going in another. They're going to burn up fuel in that bus."

"Yes, sir."

He said, "I see that beside that, you've got a van that the crusade team is going to travel in along behind that 18-wheeler."

I said, "Yes, sir, that's right."

He said, "I guess the rest of you who have to be in Tulsa most of the time are going to have to fly in and out of Tulsa to be in the meetings?"

I said, "Yes, sir, that's right."

The preacher said, "How in the world do you expect to do that in this day and age? Don't you know every ministry in the country is in trouble? Don't you know we haven't got the money to do those kinds of things? We've had to cut back in our outreach programs. We've had to cut back on everything in our ministry because the money's tight."

I said, "I'm going to tell you something, brother. God is my source, and God is still the same God He always was. He doesn't ever change. I'm going to see what God said, and I'm going to do what God said."

That is being "at peace." "At peace" is not listening to those who say things like, "Oh, you can't do *that*, brother. That's never been done in this church. Nobody's ever attempted a program like that!" I'm going to be at peace and do what God told me to do.

They've only told Fred Price about 500

times that he couldn't possibly do what he's doing at Crenshaw Christian Center in Inglewood, California, which now has 12,000 members. (In fact, they've probably told him that a lot more than 500 times.)

When Dr. Roy Hicks of the Foursquare denomination was supervisor for the Oregon-Washington-Idaho-Montana-Wyoming District, a lot of people told him, "You can't do much in those little churches. You'll have to concentrate your efforts in the large towns."

He didn't listen to them. He went in there as a supervisor and began to talk to those ministers about getting acquainted with God and moving with God. Soon churches that had 40 in attendance had 400 people, and others went from 400 to 4,000. Yet some people had told him it couldn't be done.

Brother Demos Shakarian was at our Campmeeting '82. I'm sure many people told him the Full Gospel Business Men's

Fellowship International couldn't do what it has done.

And every one of you has been told that you can't do it. Some of you listened. You were going around trying to line up with God, all out of peace, making a confession of faith one day and being upset the next. Maybe you didn't admit it to anybody, but you were. You weren't at peace. And you wonder why you're not prosperous.

Do you remember what our text said? "Acquaint now yourself with Him [agree with God and show yourself to be conformed to His will] and be at peace; by that [YOU SHALL PROSPER AND GREAT] GOOD SHALL COME TO YOU."

You shall prosper and great good shall come to you. How? By getting acquainted with God; finding out who and what He is; learning of all the inheritance He's given us; lining up with His will; being at peace; not allowing anything anybody says to bother you; knowing what God said; and keeping a smile, praising the Lord, and marching on for Jesus. The decision rests with you about how much of the inheritance you enjoy.

Someone may say to you, "Oh, you're another one of *them* . . . ." That's all right. Just walk on. Walk on in the Spirit. Walk on in the authority of Jesus' Name. Walk on in the power and might of the heavenly Father. Watch the supernatural flow as you walk day by day and step by step.

"The darkness of night shall turn to the brightness of day, and the supernatural light of the power of God shall lift you and hurl you into the good and great things that belong to you, because I have already given it to you, saith the Lord."

This is what the Spirit was saying down on the inside of me; I decided it was good for you, so I just spoke it out. I wasn't prophesying.

God gave me this message when I was

sitting in church one Sunday morning two weeks before Campmeeting '82. It was the first time I got to go to my home church in Tulsa all summer, because we had been out preaching. We had a very good speaker that Sunday. He made one statement — "Get acquainted with God" — and I don't know a thing he said the rest of the sermon, because the Spirit of God began to speak to me. I started writing. The Spirit of God said, "That's your opening sermon for Campmeeting."

Then at Campmeeting, as I was listening to my Father tell how the Spirit had told him, "The key word of the Campmeeting is the supernatural," the Lord said to me, "That's it. The key to the supernatural is to get acquainted with God."

It's simple. It's not complex. Just get acquainted with God.

You first must get acquainted with Him through salvation. You don't have to do anything or give up anything to be saved — just come to Him as you are.

Others may be acquainted with God through salvation, but not through the in-filling of the Holy Spirit. Get acquainted with God in this way. He will be real to you and will minister to you. You will not be disappointed.

Then God made everything. He made:

* The planets and stars
* The land and sea
* The plants and trees
* All kinds of animals
* People (Adam and Eve)

Genesis 1

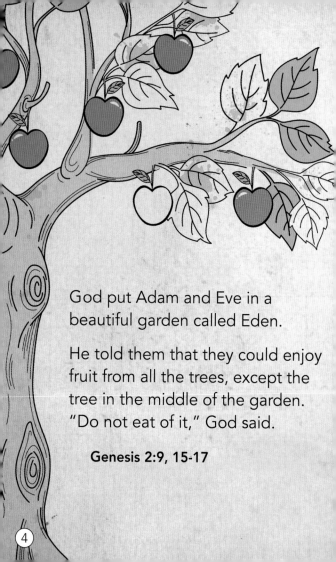

God put Adam and Eve in a
beautiful garden called Eden.

He told them that they could enjoy
fruit from all the trees, except the
tree in the middle of the garden.
"Do not eat of it," God said.

Genesis 2:9, 15-17

But sadly, Adam and Eve disobeyed God. They decided to eat the fruit that God had told them not to eat.

That's how sin came into the world and made everything go wrong! Sin brought sickness, sadness and death.

Genesis 3:1-19

The people's sin became like a thick cloud between them and God.

God who is pure and holy could not even look at sin, and so He could no longer come close to the people He loved.

Isaiah 59:2, Habakkuk 1:13

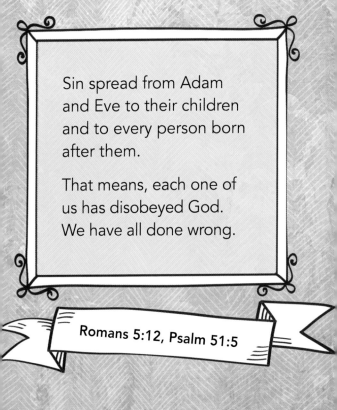

Sin spread from Adam and Eve to their children and to every person born after them.

That means, each one of us has disobeyed God. We have all done wrong.

Romans 5:12, Psalm 51:5

But God loved us so much that He sent Jesus His Son to earth so that He could take away our sin.

Jesus came to show people how much God loves them. But instead of listening to Him and following God's ways, people hurt Jesus and nailed Him to a cross.

While Jesus was on the cross, God put the sin of the whole world on Him.

Jesus took the punishment for everyone's sin. He died so that we can have never-ending life.

John 3:16-17, 1 Peter 2:24

Jesus died with ALL our sins
and was buried in a tomb.
That means, our sin went
to the grave with Jesus
and stayed there!

But after three days,
God brought Jesus back
to life again.

Jesus came out of the grave
and had a perfect body. He
showed Himself to His friends
and followers so they could
see that He was really alive.

Then He went back to
His Father in heaven.

**1 Peter 3:18,
1 Corinthians 15:4-5**

Because Jesus died to take away sin, He can make your heart clean. And when your heart is clean, God's Spirit can live inside of you and make you a part of God's family.

Would you like to become a child of God?

This is something *you must decide*!

Jesus can make you new

If you want to ask Jesus to make your heart new, here is a prayer you can pray:

Dear Jesus,

I know that I have sinned and done wrong. You are the only one who can take away my sin. Please forgive me and make my heart pure.

Amen

You can also use your own words, and even if they don't come out the way you want them to, Jesus sees your heart.

God doesn't just take away our sin. He makes us new on the inside. He gives us a heart that wants to do right.

The heart that the Lord makes new is not the heart that beats in your chest.

It is the unseen heart inside of you that connects you to God.

John 14:20

The Holy Spirit in you

God, Jesus and the Holy Spirit are one.

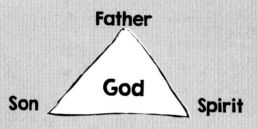

Father

God

Son   **Spirit**

When Jesus went back to His Father in heaven, He sent the Holy Spirit to come and live in the hearts of those who believe in Him.

The Holy Spirit ...

* in us is a sign that we are saved.
* helps us to worship God.
* gives us power to do what is right.
* helps us to understand the Bible.
* guides us to know God's plan for us.

John 14:16-17 and 1 John 3:24

Bible verses about being saved

Jesus told him, "I am the way, the truth, and the life. No one can come to the Father except through Me." **John 14:6**

• •

Jesus replied, "I tell you the truth, unless you are born again, you cannot see the Kingdom of God." **John 3:3**

• •

If you confess with your mouth that Jesus is Lord and believe in your heart that God raised Him from the dead, you will be saved. **Romans 10:9**

• •

"I will give you a new heart and put a new spirit in you." **Ezekiel 36:26**

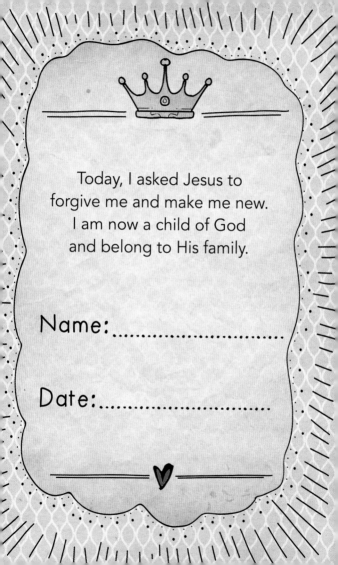

Today, I asked Jesus to
forgive me and make me new.
I am now a child of God
and belong to His family.

Name: ....

Date: ....

Your name has been written in the Book of Life, which is kept safe in heaven.

Revelation 3:5

From today, you have a new life that will carry on forever and ever. When your time on earth is up, you will go live with God in His home.

John 14:1-3

How will your life be different?

Most things will stay the same. You may not even feel any different.

But a very important change has happened in your life. You have been born into God's family, which means you've been born again (a second time).

John 1:12-13

When God looks at you now, He sees you as perfect, even when you do something wrong. God will always love you just as you are. All He wants is that you ask Him to forgive you.

You now have the Holy Spirit living in you to help you do what is right and good. As you follow God's way, you will want to do things that please Jesus instead of doing wrong things.

You belong to God now, and no one can snatch you away from Him! If you ever doubt that you are really a child of God, remember that your name has been written in God's Book. How you feel won't change that, and it doesn't change God's love for you!

Hebrews 10:14, 1 John 1:9, John 10:28

Grow in your faith

When a seed is dry, it's as though the seed is dead. But when that seed is covered with soil and watered, it begins to grow.

In the same way, Jesus has put the seed of eternal life in your heart and He wants you to grow and become more like Him.

The Holy Spirit is like water, giving us eternal life; and God is like the sun, shining His goodness into our hearts.

John 4:14, 2 Corinthians 4:6

Read the Bible

The Bible is God's written Word. It has everything He wants us to know.

* The Bible will help you get to know God better and love Him more.
* The Bible will help you to know right from wrong.
* The Bible will help you to grow strong in your faith.
* The Bible will help you to know what God wants you to do.
* The promises God gives you in the Bible will encourage you!

Psalm 119:105, 2 Timothy 3:16

Pray

Talk to God as often and as much as you want. He loves to hear your prayers! Tell Him about everything that's going on in your life. Thank Him for all He has done for you, and also pray for others. You can pray ...

* any time
* anywhere and
* about anything.

When you ask God for something, believe that He will hear your prayer. Then, keep on praying, and patiently wait for God to answer.

**Philippians 4:6,
1 John 5:14-15**

Stick together

Try to get together with others
who love Jesus.

A church group is the best place
to meet friends and be encouraged.

Children's church or
Sunday school is
a great place to
worship God and
learn about
the Bible.

Hebrews 10:24-25

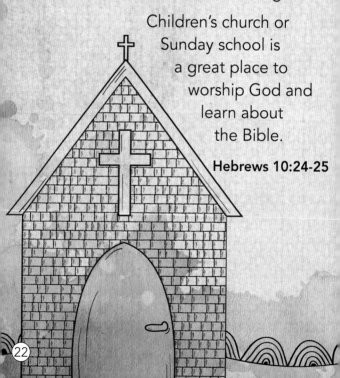

Tell others

Jesus wants us to tell others about Him. You could use this little book to tell your friends how Jesus saved you.

Important things to know:

* God loves us.
* We have all sinned (done wrong).
* Jesus died for our sin. He took the blame for our sin.
* Jesus wants to save us from sin and give us eternal life.
* To be saved, you must ask Jesus to forgive you and make you new.

2 Timothy 4:2, Romans 3:23-24, Psalm 51:10

Other important things to know

God has a special plan for you. He uses things that happen in your life to help you become more like Him, and to work out His plan for you.

People will start noticing changes in your life. Like a tree that bears fruit, your life will start showing fruit that comes from your heart.

"The Holy Spirit produces this kind of fruit in our lives: love, joy, peace, patience, kindness, goodness, faithfulness, gentleness, and self-control."

Galatians 5:22-23

And there is more exciting news!

Romans 8:28, John 15:16

Jesus told us that He is coming back soon. When He comes back, we will see Him in the clouds. Those who belong to Jesus will go up to be with Him. We will have perfect bodies in heaven and be so happy that we can't begin to imagine what it will be like!

We will also receive a beautiful crown from Jesus, and each one of us will receive a reward for the good we have done on earth.

Revelation 22:12,
1 Thessalonians 4:16-17

Bible verses about ...

* **Prayer**
  Luke 11:9-13

* **The Bible**
  Psalm 119:9-11
  Psalm 119:105
  Romans 15:4

* **God**
  Revelation 1:8

* **Jesus**
  Mark 1:10-11
  Philippians 2:6-11

* **The Holy Spirit**
  John 16:5-15

* **The Church**
  Acts 2:42-47

* **Heaven**
  Isaiah 66:1

* **Temptation**
  James 1:2-4
  James 1:13
  I Corinthians 10:13

* **Wisdom**
  James 1:5

* **Faith**
  Hebrews 11:1
  Hebrews 11:6
  James 1:3
  Romans 10:17

* **Guidance**
  Proverbs 3:5-6
  Isaiah 30:21
  Psalm 48:14

Where to find it in the Bible

* **Creation**
Genesis 1

* **Ten Commandments**
Exodus 20:1–17

* **The Shepherd's Psalm**
Psalm 23

* **Jesus' birth**
Matthew 1:18–25
Luke 2

* **Jesus' death**
Mark 15
John 19

* **Jesus' rising**
John 20
Luke 24

* **Jesus' ascension**
Acts 1:6–11

* **Jesus' return**
John 14:1–4

* **The Lord's Supper**
Matthew 26:26–29

* **Beatitudes**
Matthew 5:3–12

* **Love**
1 Corinthians 13

* **The Armor of God**
Ephesians 6:10–18

* **Gifts of the Spirit**
Romans 12:6–8,
1 Corinthians 12:8–10

Bible verses for when you are ...

* **Sad**
  Psalm 147:3
  Psalm 34:17–18

* **Discouraged**
  Psalm 42:5
  Deuteronomy 31:8
  Isaiah 41:10

* **Afraid**
  Isaiah 41:13
  John 14:27
  Psalm 91:11

* **Worried**
  Philippians 4:6–7
  1 Peter 5:7
  Matthew 6:25–34

* **Lonely**
  Psalm 68:6
  Deuteronomy 31:6

* **Angry**
  Proverbs 15:1
  Ephesians 4:26
  James 1:19–20
  Proverbs 12:16

* **Tempted**
  1 Corinthians 10:13

* **In trouble**
  Nahum 1:7

* **Feeling guilty**
  1 John 1:9
  Isaiah 43:25

* **Feeling unloved**
  Jeremiah 1:5
  Jeremiah 31:3

Making a salvation bracelet

This bracelet uses colors to remind us of what it means to be saved.
(Use pony beads and a nylon cord.)

Dark – reminds us of sin.

Romans 3:23

Red – reminds us of Jesus' blood, when He died for our sin.

1 John 1:7

White – reminds us of a clean heart.

Psalm 51:7

Green – reminds us to grow and become more like Jesus.

2 Peter 3:18

Gold – reminds us of our eternal life in heaven.

John 14:2

The prayer of Jesus

Jesus taught us to pray like this:

"Our Father in heaven,
may Your name be kept holy.
May Your Kingdom come soon.
May Your will be done on earth,
as it is in heaven.

Give us today the food we need, and
forgive us our sins, as we have forgiven
those who sin against us.
And don't let us yield to temptation,
but rescue us from the evil one."

Amen.

Matthew 6:9-13

Notes

Copyright © 2019 by Christian Art Kids,
an imprint of Christian Art Publishers,
PO Box 1599, Vereeniging, 1930, RSA

© 2019
First edition 2019

Cover designed by Christian Art Kids
Designed by Christian Art Kids

Images used under license from Shutterstock.com

Printed in China

ISBN 978-1-4321-2966-8

19 20 21 22 23 24 25 26 27 28 – 11 10 9 8 7 6 5 4 3 2

Printed in Shenzhen, China
August 2019
Print Run: 100553